DINOSAURS

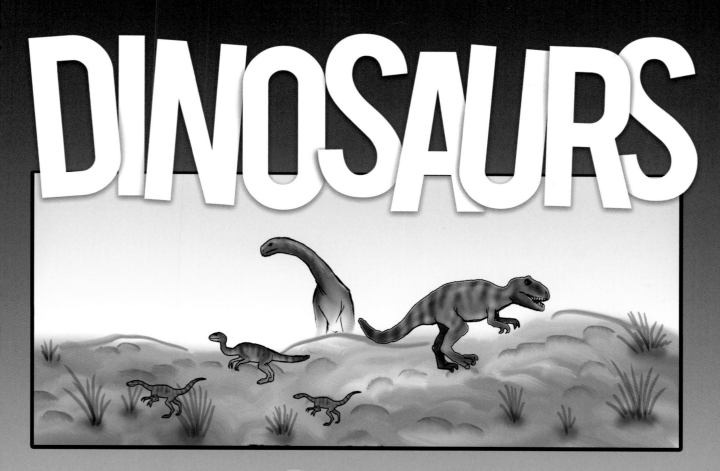

for **Little Kids** Where did they go?

KEN HAM

illustrated by Bill Looney

First printing: June 2019
Second printing: October 2019

Master Books®. P.O. Box 726. Green Forest. AR 72638

Master Books® is a division of the New Leaf Publishing Group. Inc.

ISBN: 978-1-68344-199-1
ISBN: 978-1-61458-717-0 (digital)
Library of Congress Number: 2019941756

Illustrated by Bill Looney

Unless otherwise noted. Scripture quotations are from the New King
James Version of the Bible.

Please consider requesting that a copy of this volume be purchased by
your local library system.

Printed in the South Korea

Please visit our website for other great titles:
www.masterbooks.com

For information regarding author interviews.
please contact the publicity department at (870) 438-5288.

Master
Books®
A Division of New Leaf Publishing Group
www.masterbooks.com

Hello kids – come on in. Get ready for some fun!
Follow me deep inside my Dinosaurium.

Imagine you met Adam, the very first man,
back when he named the animals as part of God's plan.
And after he had named the creatures God gave life,
he saw that there were none like him, so God made him a wife.

DINOSAURS

CREATED
KINDS

DAY 5

BIRDS

FLYING
REPTILES
& MAMMALS

SEA
CREATURES

DAY 6

LAND
ANIMALS

DINOSAURS

BIRDS

FLYING REPTILES & MAMMALS

SEA CREATURES

LAND ANIMALS

So Adam called her Eve. The Garden was their home,
with all of the animal kinds that flew or crept or roamed.
There were many kinds of creatures in Eden, after all,
from great big ones down to those that were very small.

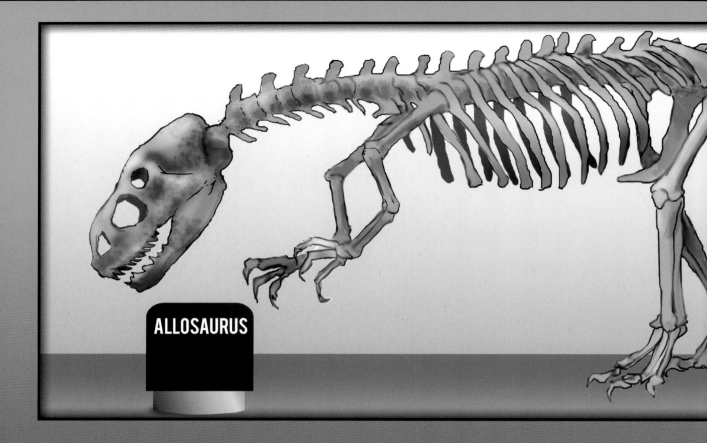

ALLOSAURUS

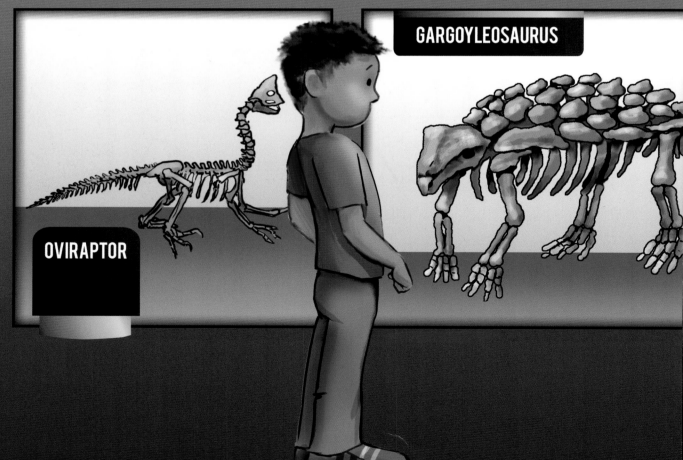

GARGOYLEOSAURUS

OVIRAPTOR

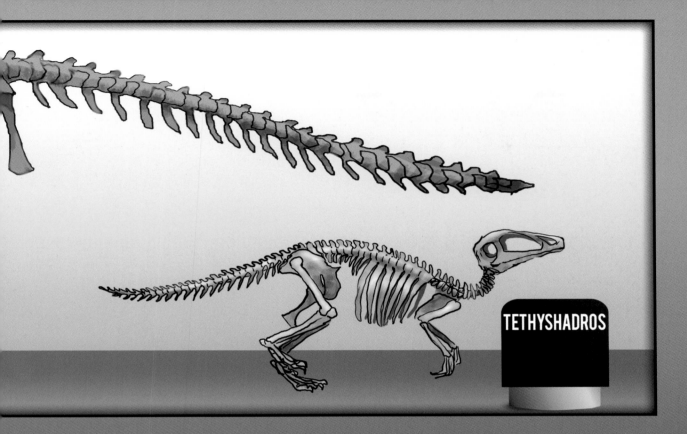

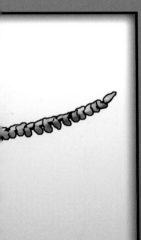

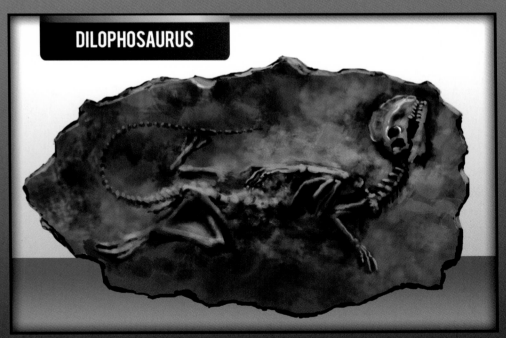

TETHYSHADROS

DILOPHOSAURUS

And some of them were what we call dinosaurs today,
but back when Adam named them, it wasn't that way.
I do love dinosaurs! I'll bet you do as well,
but where their name came from is a story to tell.

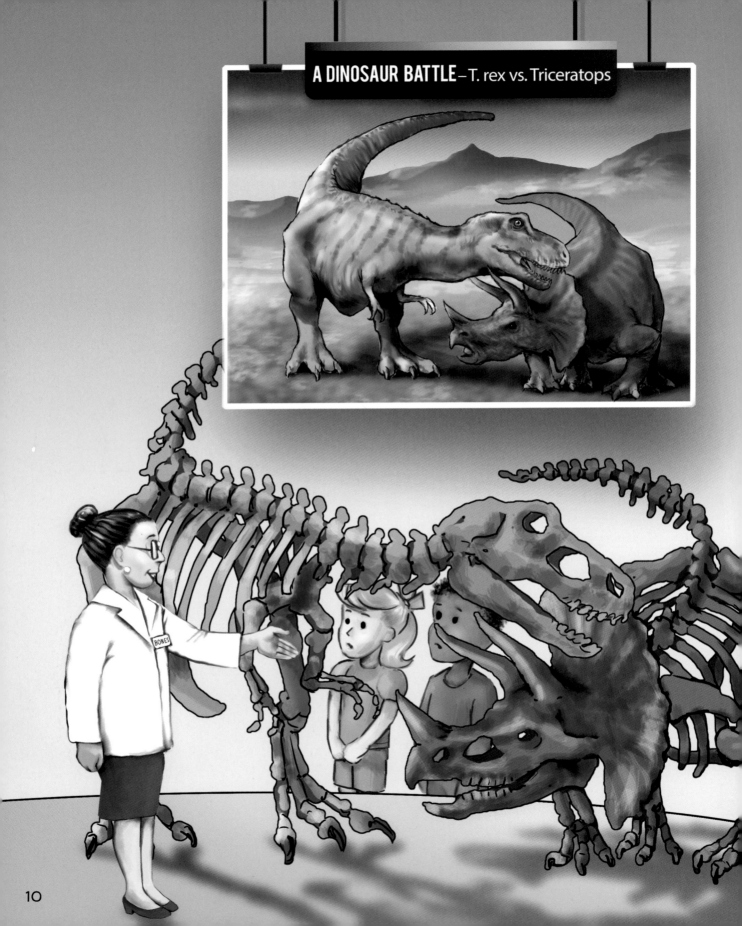

A DINOSAUR BATTLE—T. rex vs. Triceratops

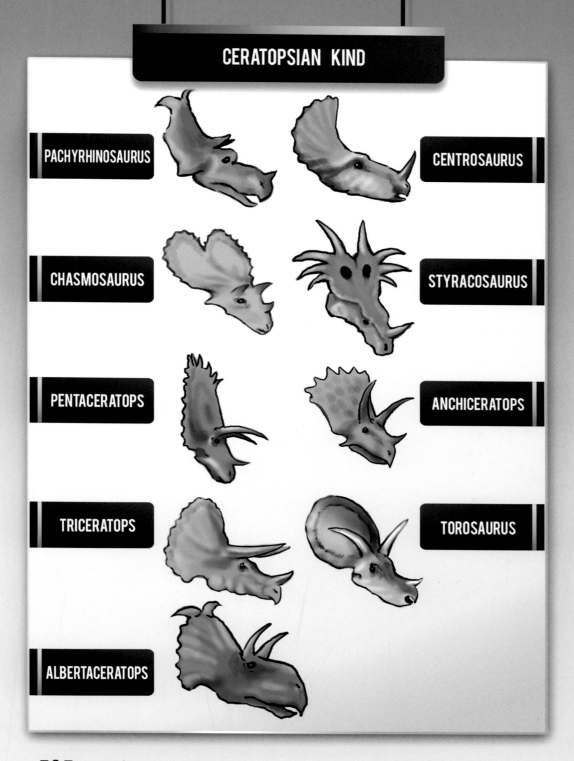

CERATOPSIAN KIND

PACHYRHINOSAURUS

CENTROSAURUS

CHASMOSAURUS

STYRACOSAURUS

PENTACERATOPS

ANCHICERATOPS

TRICERATOPS

TOROSAURUS

ALBERTACERATOPS

If I could name the dinosaurs, this is what I'd do.
I'd give them lots of funny names, how about you?
Like Xingerdat, Slossertring, Ballermut, and more.
Can you think of a funny name? How 'bout three or four?

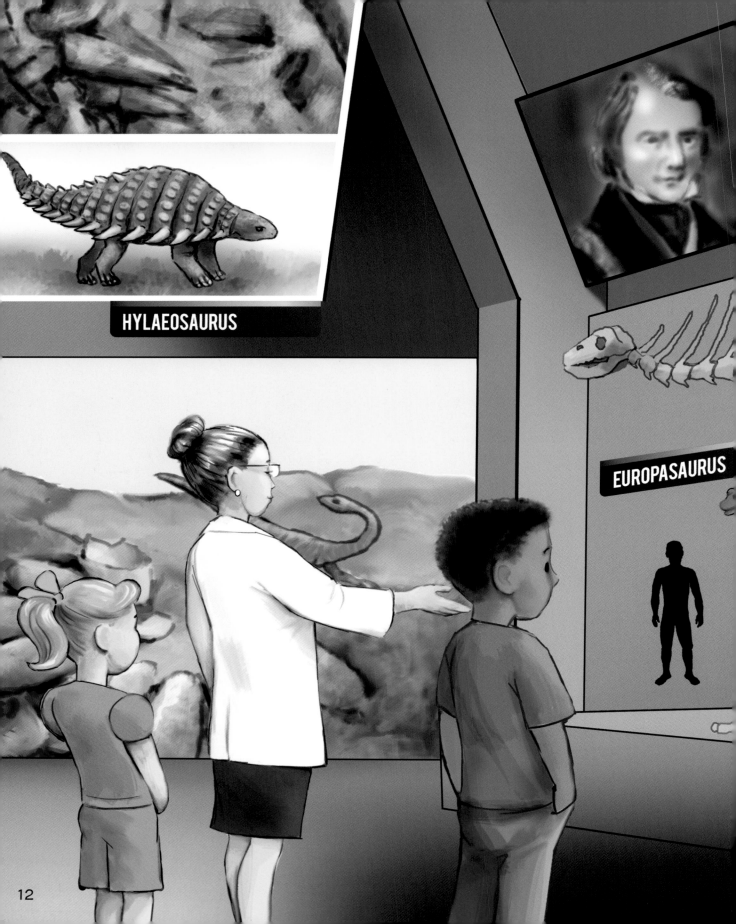

HYLAEOSAURUS

EUROPASAURUS

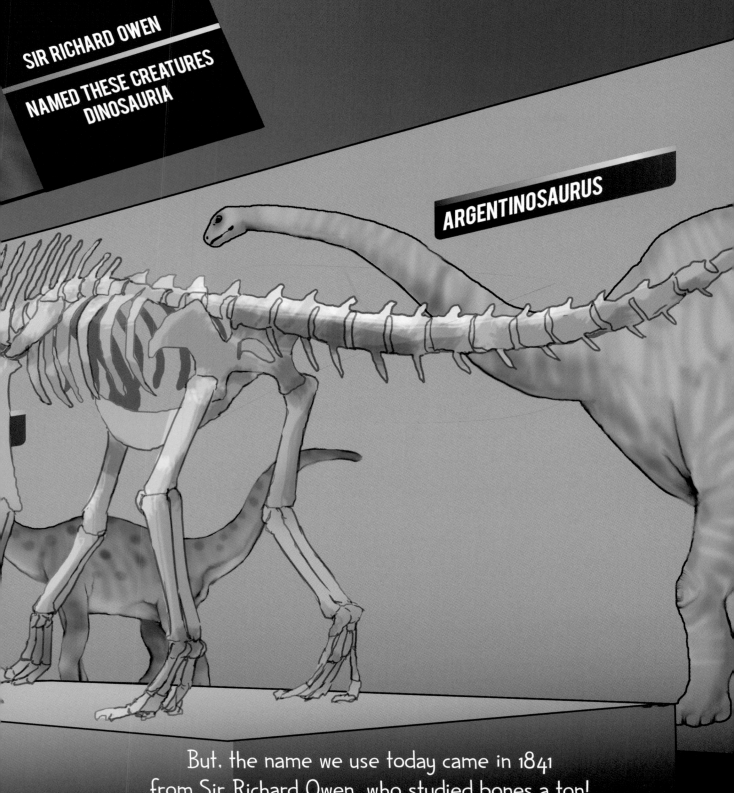

SIR RICHARD OWEN

NAMED THESE CREATURES
DINOSAURIA

ARGENTINOSAURUS

But, the name we use today came in 1841
from Sir Richard Owen, who studied bones a ton!
He found fossils in England like none he'd seen before.
They looked like fearful lizards, so he called them dinosaurs.

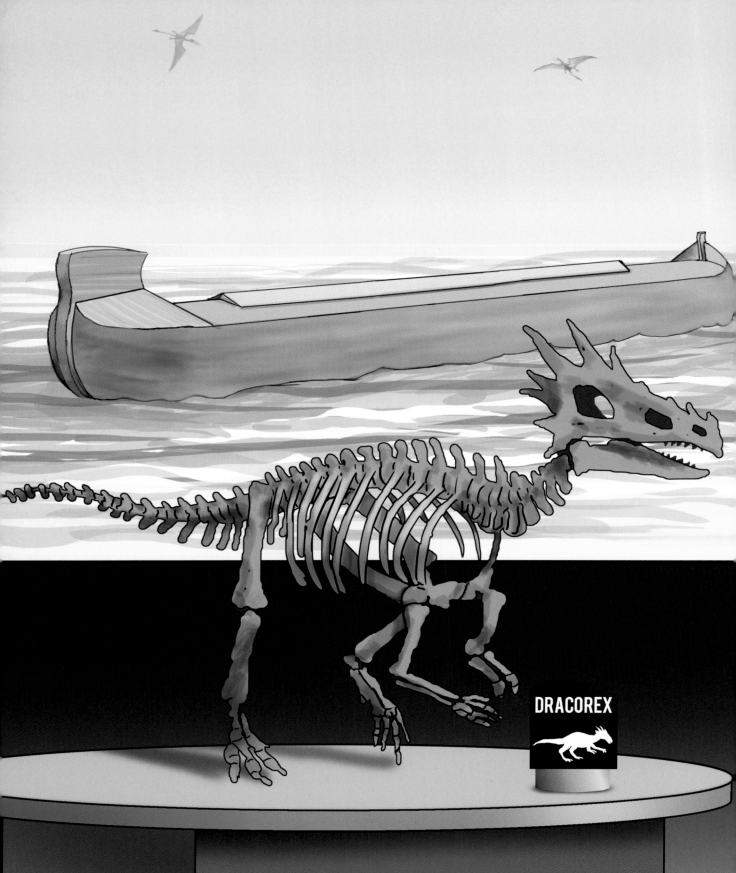

All those terrible lizards died so very long ago,
that people had forgotten them; they just didn't know.
They once were called dragons—it's no great mystery.
Yes, you can find dragon legends all through history.

DRAGON

UTAHRAPTOR

STEGOSAURUS

PARASAUROLOPHUS

Yes, I love dinosaurs, and they're no mystery.
It's such fun for us to learn how their name came to be.
And by reading the Bible, written for you and me,
we learn the truth, even of dinosaur history.

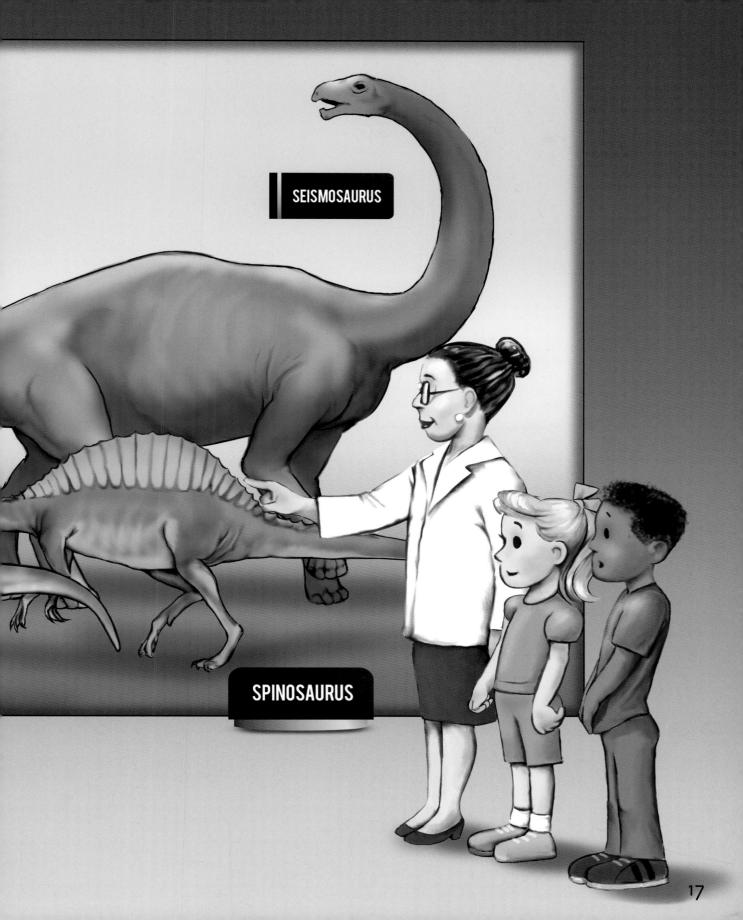

SEISMOSAURUS

SPINOSAURUS

17

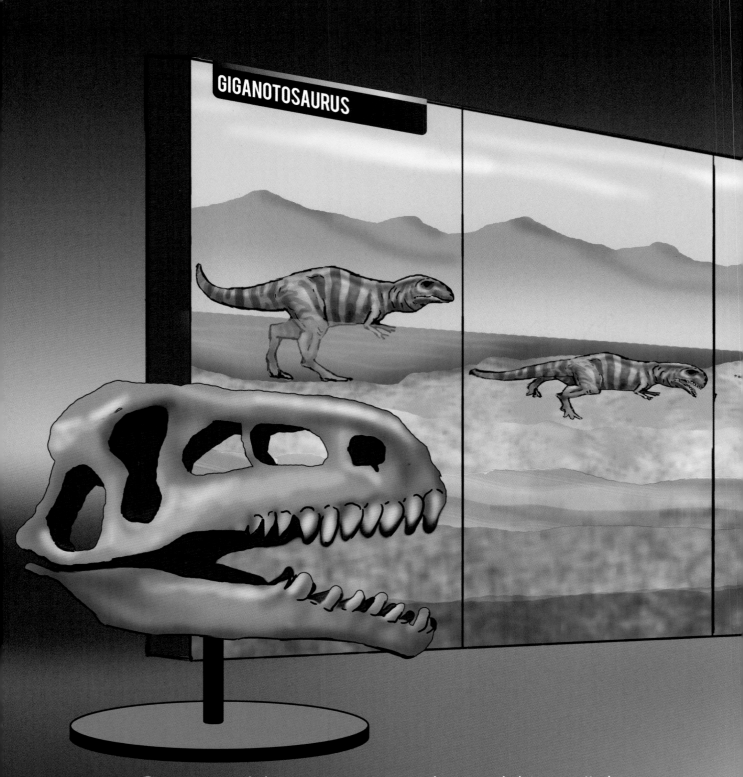

But where did they all go you ask, why did they all die?
The answer is in Genesis. God's Word tells us why.
Most of them were washed away, drowned in the Great Flood.
They were buried underneath lots and lots of mud.

That is why their bones are found covered by the ground,
petrified and fossilized, all the world around.
Just remember that they're only thousands of years old.
No, it isn't millions as we are sometimes told.

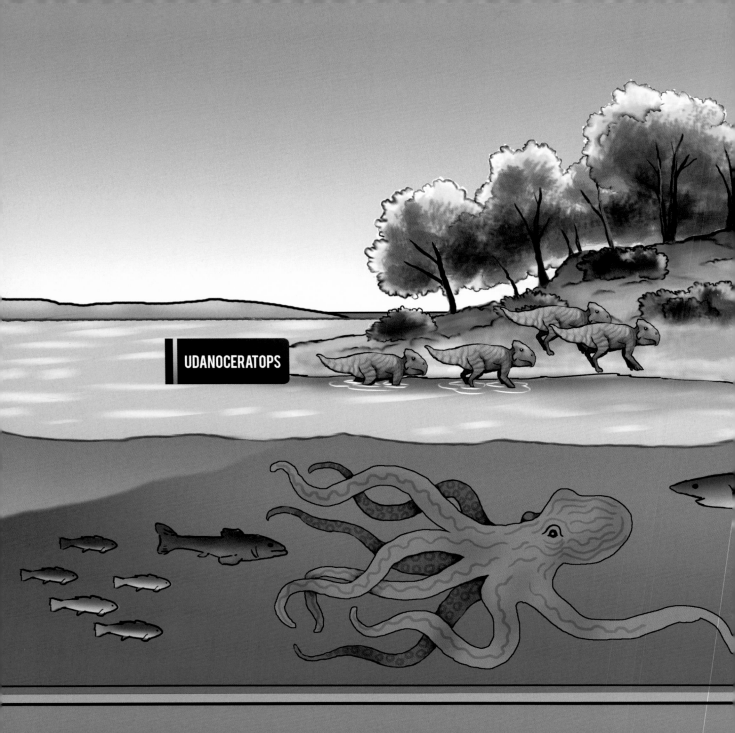

UDANOCERATOPS

A few of them survived the Flood, and lived in olden days,
with two of every other land animal God had made.
They left the Ark when Noah did. The world they knew was gone.
So those legendary dragons died off as time went on.

NOTHRONYCHUS

I wish that dinosaurs were here and didn't have to die.
It's all because of sin, you see. That's the reason why.
Adam chose to disobey, and that's when death began,
but God loves us all so much, He had a special plan.

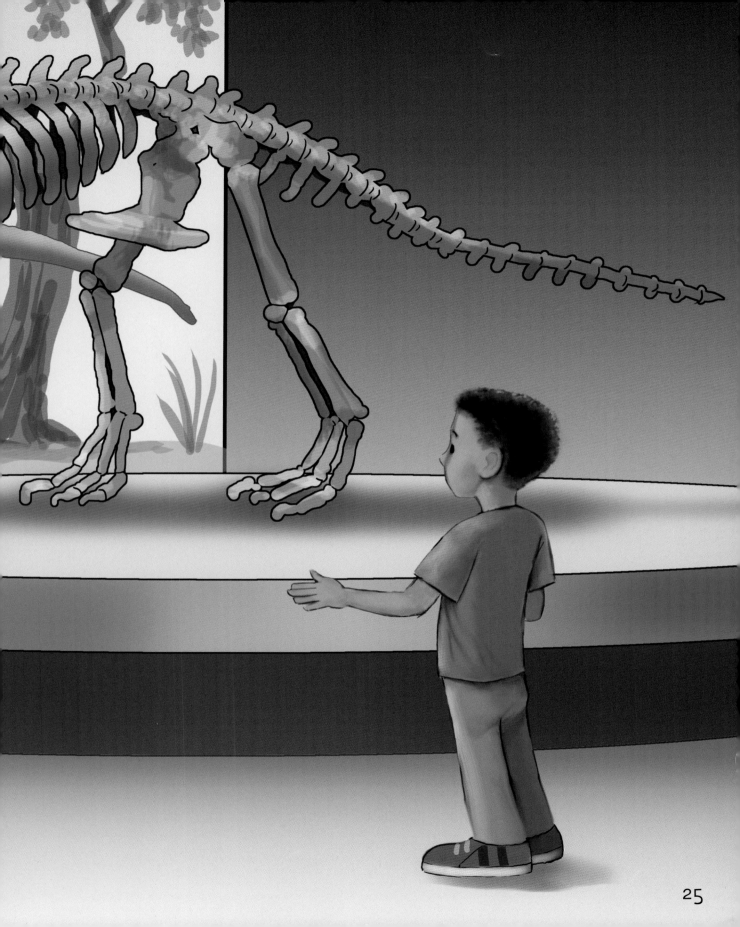

He sent His own son, Jesus, who loved mankind —and then,
took the death upon Himself that Adam's sin brought in.
He gave His life upon a Cross that day His blood was shed,
but on the third day in the grave, He rose up from the dead.

27

Now, all who trust in Jesus and confess Him as their Lord
will have their sins forgiven—their hope will be restored.
For one day He promises that death will be no more.
We'll live with Him in heaven—that's what our Lord came for!

I Love Dinosaurs!

Bambiraptor
[BAM-bee-rap-tor]
Discovered in 1993 by a 14-year-old fossil hunter in Montana. It was 3 feet in length and named for a popular Disney character. It's unknown how large an adult would have been.

Gasparinisaura
[GAS-paw-re-nee-sawr-uh]
Found in 1992 in Argentina. It was around 3 to 4 feet in length, with very large eyes and long hind feet. Most fossils discovered were not adults.

Wannanosaurus
[wah-NAN-o-sawr-us]
Revealed in China in 1977. This very small dinosaur was around 2 feet long, with indications that the fossil found was an adult.

Lesothosaurus
[LESS-sew-tow-SAWR-us]
At just over 6 feet long as an adult with a small skull, this South African dinosaur had a short, pointed snout. Its back teeth included some that were leaf-shaped, and it had 12 sharp teeth in the front.

Microceratus
[MY-cro-SER-a-us]
Among the smallest of the dinosaurs at around 2 feet long and less than 15 pounds as an adult, its name means "small-horned." Found in Asia, it has similarities to other horned dinosaurs.

Udanoceratops
[oo-DON-o-SER-a-tops]
This dinosaur was 13 feet long and less than 6 feet tall. Uncovered in Mongolia, with fossils also found in China, it had strong, curved jaws and long hind legs.

Giganotosaurus
[jig-uh-NO-tah-sawr-us]
At just over 40 feet long, its fossil was discovered in Patagonia. Scientists think it could have run at around 30 miles per hour. Tracks of this dinosaur, as well as teeth, have been found.

Spinosaurus
[spy-NO-sawr-us]
This dinosaur with a long thin skull made North Africa its home and grew to almost 60 feet in length. Its bones were first found in Egypt in the early 1900s.

Utahraptor
[YOU-tah-rap-tor]
At over 20 feet long and more than 1,000 pounds, this adult fossil was first found in Utah in 1975. It is known by the over 9-inch curved claws on its hind feet.

Seismosaurus
[SIES-mo-SAWR-us] Among the huge sauropod dinosaurs, this one is still considered one of the largest at 150 feet in length. Discovered in New Mexico, it may have weighed up to 100 tons, with a neck 40 feet long.

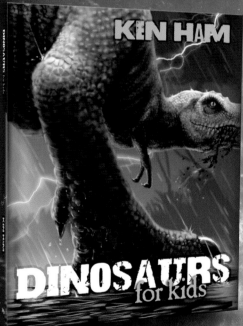

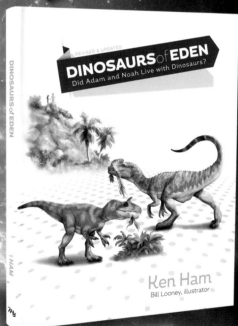

DINOSAURS FOR KIDS

Ken Ham

Within these pages kids will uncover the facts about dinosaur history from the creation to recent discoveries. Let Ken Ham take you on a journey through time to explore these awesome wonders of God's design.

978-0-89051-555-6 **$14.99** U.S.

DINOSAURS OF EDEN

Ken Ham

Fully revised and updated, this beloved classic will take you on a breathtaking trip across time to the biblical foundation of dinosaurs. This captivating adventure by Ken Ham explores the Garden of Eden, the exciting days of Noah's Flood, and the Tower of Babel. You'll learn the true history of the earth, and discover the very meaning and purpose of life!

978-0-89051-902-8 **$15.99** U.S.

Available where fine books are sold.   MasterBooks.com